Achille's Proficiency Guide
For the Eastern Star Degree

ISBN-13:
978-1480218765

Conventon & Associates Agency, LLC
©2012 Publishing Company: C&A Publishing
Lead Publisher: Kennedy Achille

Conventon Associates
Publishing as C & A Publishing
Hollywood, Florida, 33020

This book belongs to

_____

Conventon & Associates Agency, LLC

Congratulations, you have just embarked on a great journey to a destination only you can set. I want you to understand a few things that may help you become the best member you can ever be. The first thing I want you to do is to never forget who you are. Become cautious of your public actions and the way you represent yourself. This comes with two difficult tasks to accomplish. The first is representing yourself, and the second is representing your Chapter. Never forget that you do not need to display any Masonic symbols to show your love for the organization, your heart will take care of all of that. The world is yours and is ready for the taking. Use your tools to positively influence the minds in the community. Recruit individuals that want to contribute greatly to your organization. Recruit individuals that will work just as hard as you do. We all joined an organization to better ourselves in one-way or another. As a member, leave behind a positive impact on the people you encounter. So far, you left one on me and I thank you for that. To prevent further negativity in the Masonic order live by the obligations for which you took an oath on. Stay loyal to the fundamental purpose of your organization and never forget your teachings. You now have the necessary tools to combat tough situations in life.

What strengths will you bring to the Order?	What weaknesses do you want to improve on?

Strengths

Weakness

Conventon & Associates Agency, LLC

1

How many officers make up a chapter?
A. 3
B. 4
C. 8
D. 9

2

How many points make up the
Eastern Star?
A. 4
B. 5
C. 6
D. 7

3

What point of the Eastern Star does
ADAH represent?
A. 2
B. 3
C. 1

4

A. What color represents Ruth?

5

ADAH is the daughter of
A. Solomon
B. Boaz
C. Abraham
D. Jephthah

6

What color is NOT represented in the
Eastern Star?
A. Red
B. Orange
C. White
D. Blue

7

What shape is the center of the
Eastern Star?
A. Octagon
B. Hexagon
C. Pentagon
D. Cube

Total Score:

Total Possible Score: 7

Section 1

The first point of the Eastern Star

ADAH, the daughter of Jephtha

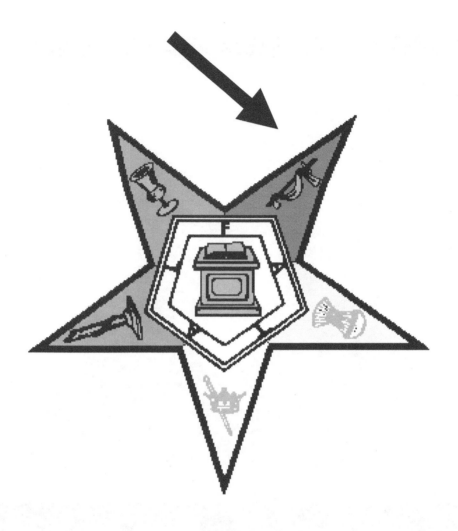

The first point is (PROVIDED BY INSTRUCTOR)
Color: (PROVIDED BY INSTRUCTOR)

Conventon & Associates Agency, LLC

ADAH-To make known to all…. (PROVIDED BY INSTRUCTOR)

Name	Point of Star	Color	Emblem	Characteristics

Conventon & Associates Agency, LLC

Define each characteristic in your own words and explain them to your instructor.

Conventon & Associates Agency, LLC

Draw the emblems that represent points of the Eastern Star

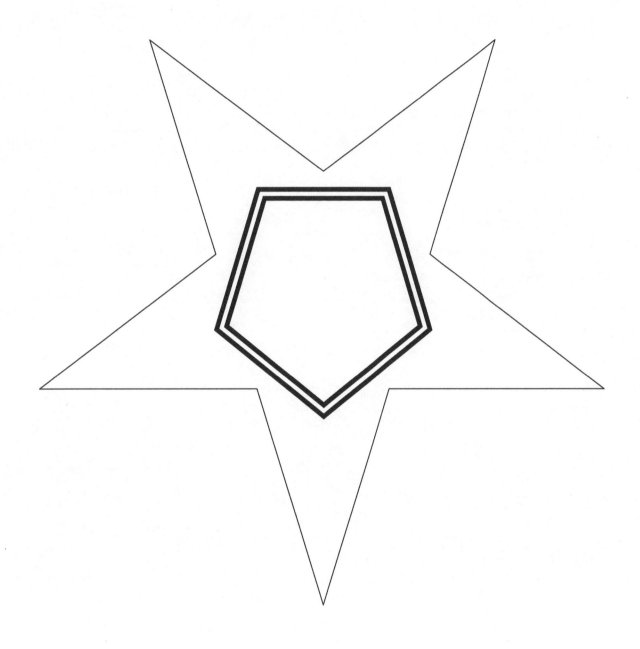

Conventon & Associates Agency, LLC

Notes

Conventon & Associates Agency, LLC

Section 2

The second point of the Eastern Star

Conventon & Associates Agency, LLC

Ruth, Wife of Boaz

Conventon & Associates Agency, LLC

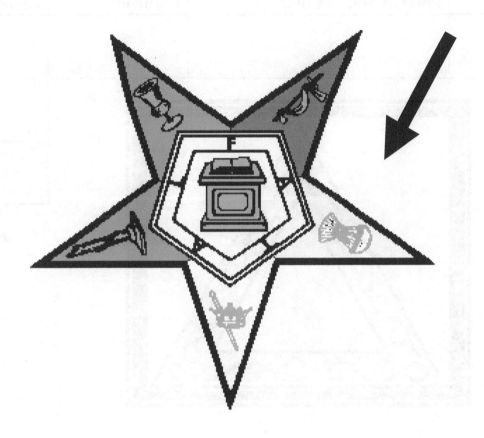

The second point is (PROVIDED BY INSTRUCTOR)

COLOR: (PROVIDED BY INSTRUCTOR)

Ruth: To make known: (PROVIDED BY INSTRUCTOR)

Name	Point of Star	Color	Emblem	Characteristics

Conventon & Associates Agency, LLC

Define each characteristic in your own words and explain them to your instructor

_____

_____

_____

_____

_____

_____

_____

_____

Conventon & Associates Agency, LLC

Draw the emblems that represent points of the Eastern Star

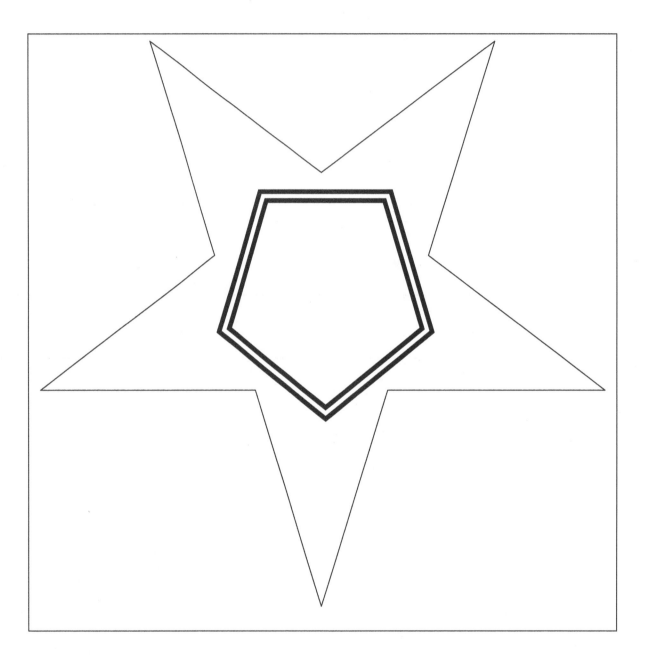

Conventon & Associates Agency, LLC

Notes:

Section 3

The third point of the Eastern Star

Conventon & Associates Agency, LLC

ESTHER

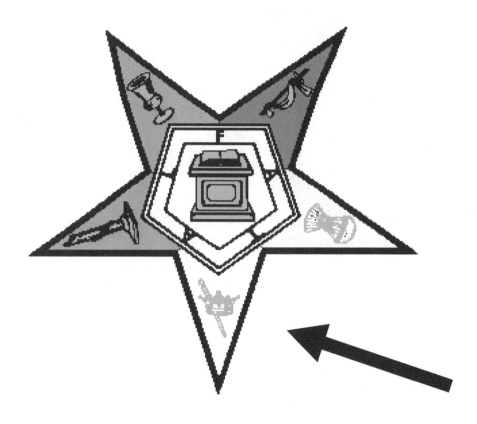

The third point is (PROVIDED BY INSTRUCTOR)

COLOR: (PROVIDED BY INSTRUCTOR)

ESTHER: To make known: (PROVIDED BY INSTRUCTOR)

Name	Point of Star	Color	Emblem	Characteristics

Conventon & Associates Agency, LLC

Define each characteristic in your own words and explain them to your instructor

Conventon & Associates Agency, LLC

Draw the emblems that represent points of the Eastern Star

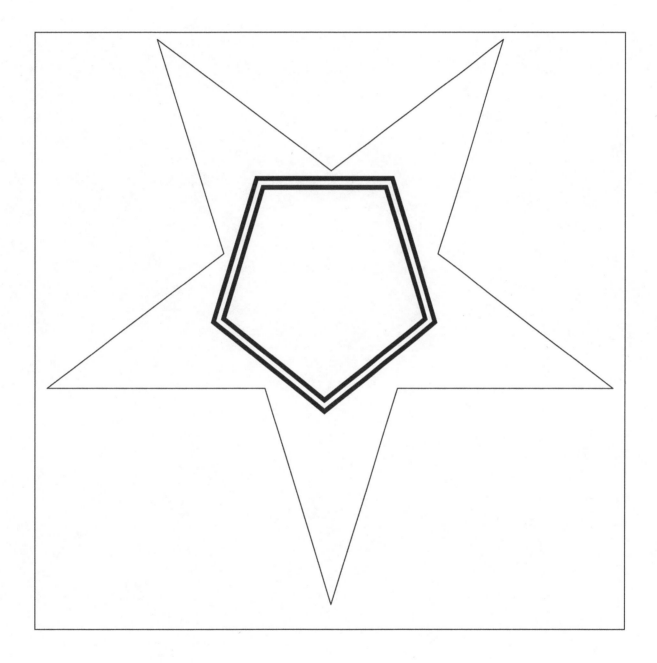

Conventon & Associates Agency, LLC

Notes:

Conventon & Associates Agency, LLC

Section 4

The fourth point of the Eastern Star

Conventon & Associates Agency, LLC

MARTHA

Conventon & Associates Agency, LLC

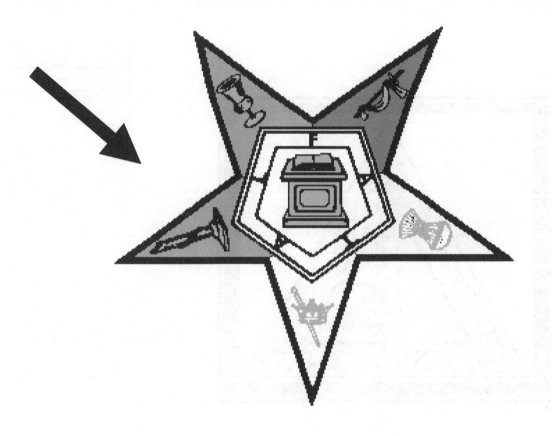

The fourth point of the Eastern Star is (PROVIDED BY INSTRUCTOR)

COLOR: (PROVIDED BY INSTRUCTOR)

Convento & Associates Agency, LLC

Name	Point of Star	Color	Emblem	Characteristics

Conventon & Associates Agency, LLC

Define each characteristic in your own words and explain them to your instructor

Conventon & Associates Agency, LLC

Draw the emblems that represent points of the Eastern Star

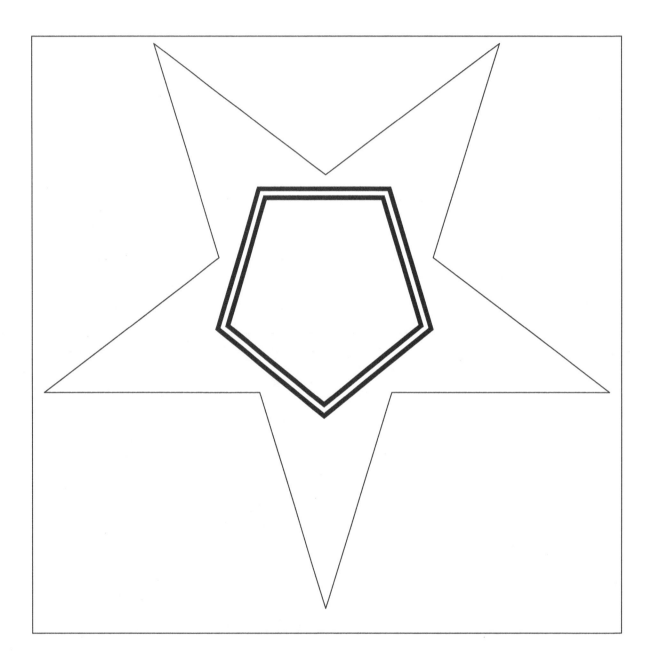

Conventon & Associates Agency, LLC

Notes:

Conventon & Associates Agency, LLC

Section 5

The fifth point of the Eastern Star

Conventon & Associates Agency, LLC

ELECTA

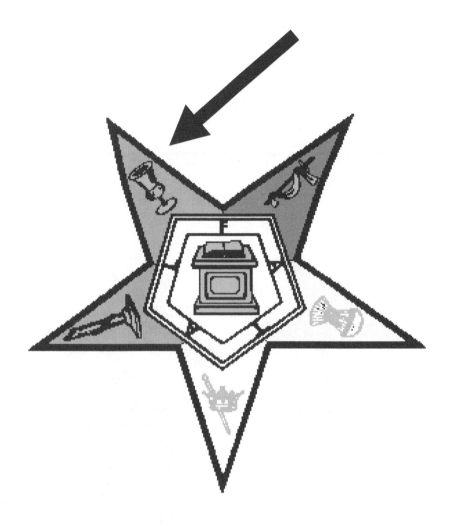

The fifth point of the Eastern Star is (PROVIDED BY INSTRUCTOR)

COLOR: (PROVIDED BY INSTRUCTOR)

Electa: To make known: (TAUGHT BY INSTRUCTOR)

Name	Point of Star	Color	Emblem	Characteristics

Conventon & Associates Agency, LLC

Define each characteristic in your own words and explain them to your instructor

Conventon & Associates Agency, LLC

Draw the emblems that represent points of the Eastern Star

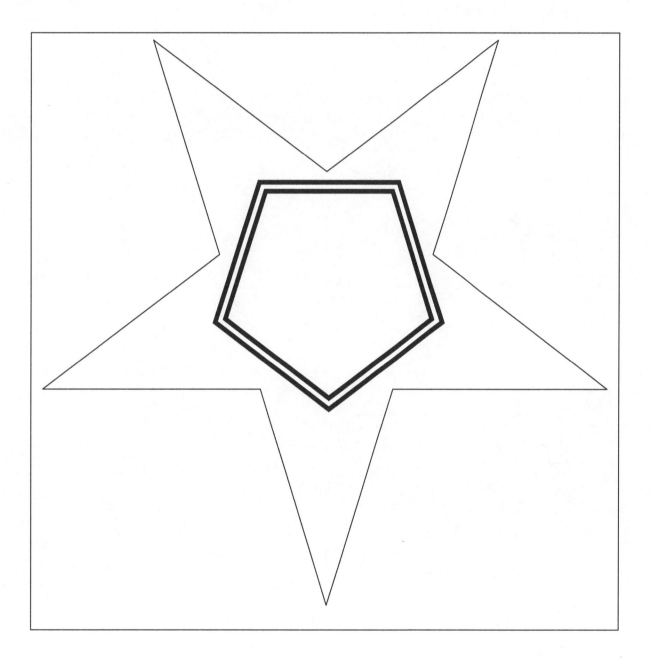

Conventon & Associates Agency, LLC

Notes:

Conventon & Associates Agency, LLC

Section 6

Eastern Star Proficiency Exam

Proficiency Exam Directions: Fill in the blanks with the accurate information as it alludes to the Eastern Star in order.

Name	Point of Star	Color	Emblem

20 possible points

List the characteristics/ 5 possible points

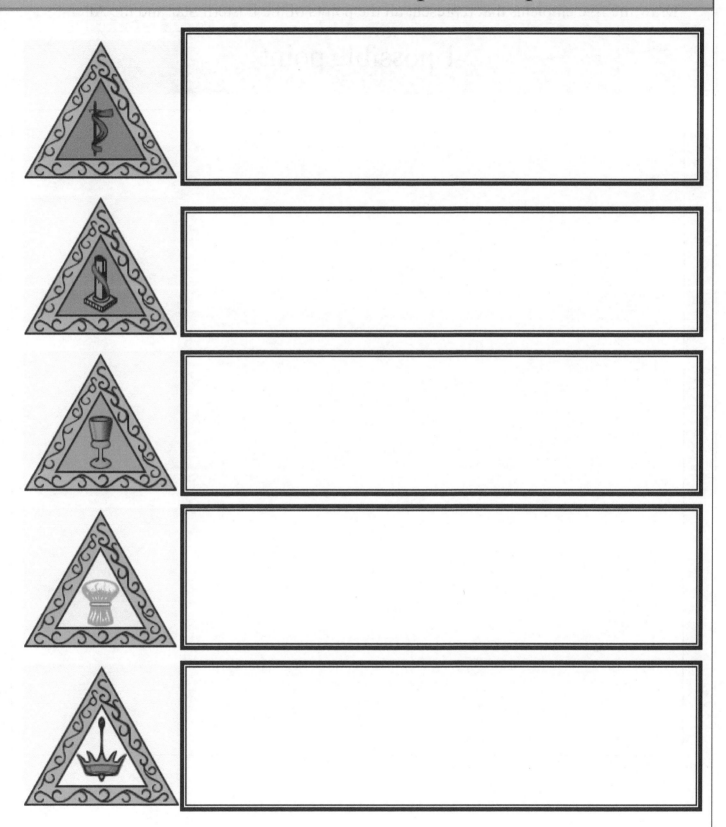

Conventon & Associates Agency, LLC

Draw the five emblems that represent all the points of the Eastern Star and the Alter

1 possible point

Conventon & Associates Agency, LLC

Chapter Jurisdiction Knowledge

1. What is the official title of your Jurisdiction?

_____

2. How many districts are in your Jurisdiction?

_____

3. How many zones are in your jurisdiction?

_____

4. Who is your current Grand Worthy Matron?

_____

5. In what year was your Grand Chapter founded?

_____

6. What is the current location of your Grand Chapter?

Street_____City_____

State_____Zip_____

7. In what month is the Grand session held in your Jurisdiction?

_____

8. How much are current annual dues?

_____

Total Possible Score: 8
Total Score:

Chapter Knowledge

1. What is the official name of your Chapter?

_____

2. What district is your Chapter in?

_____

3. What zone is your Chapter in?

_____

4. Who is your current Worthy Matron?

_____

5. In what year was your Chapter founded?

_____

6. What is the current location of your Chapter?

Street_____City_____

State_____Zip_____

Total Possible Score: 6
Total Score:

Draw the layout of the chapter and the positions of each officer.

Conventon & Associates Agency, LLC

41 possible points

Your total score:

Eastern Star Proficiency Post-Test

1

How many officers make up a chapter?
A. 3
B. 4
C. 8
D. 9

2

How many points make up the
Eastern Star?
A. 4
B. 5
C. 6
D. 7

3

What point of the Eastern Star does
ADAH represent?
A. 2
B. 3
C. 1
D. 4

4

A. What color represents Ruth?

5

ADAH is the daughter of
A. Solomon
B. Boaz
C. Abraham
D. Jephthah

6

What color is NOT represented in the
Eastern Star?
A. Red
B. Orange
C. White
D. Yellow

7

What shape is the center of the
Eastern Star?
A. Octagon
B. Hexagon
C. Pentagon
D. Cube

Total Score:

Total Possible Score: 7

Conventon & Associates Agency, LLC

This is your promise and commitment to the Order. Your promise and commitment, will be evaluated in one year from today's date

1. I promise to make an effort to help improve the order within the next year by doing the following:

2. I promise to use to the following tools of the order to help my family:

Commitment Date: /   /   /

Signature:

(TEAR THIS PAGE OUT AND GIVE TO YOUR INSTRUCTOR)

Conventon & Associates Agency, LLC

In your own words, what does this Degree mean to you?

_____

_____

_____

_____

_____

_____

_____

_____

_____

_____

_____

_____

_____

Conventon & Associates Agency, LLC

Conventon & Associates Agency, LLC

Made in United States
Cleveland, OH
02 June 2025

17418062R10031